MW00977178

This book is dedicated to those who self-abandon.

Special thanks to Billy Toulson for his encouragement and support.

Written by: Elizabeth Grace Bates

Cover Art by: Taylor Stringer & Grace Bates
&
Interior Art by: Estina Tavaziva

© 2017 Elizabeth Grace Bates
All rights reserved. No part of this book may be used or reproduced in any manner whatsoever without written permission from the author except in the case of brief quotations.

Contact the author at: bates.elizabeth.grace@gmail.com

who really
left you

leaving

being with him was like looking out the window
waiting for recess
and wishing he'd play
with you

hanging onto him was like
playing on the monkey bars for too long
left my hands stinging with blisters
burning

salty tears my lashes couldn't hold
spilled onto my wounds
and into a puddle around my knees
when the mulch caught me
and he
didn't

this is self abandonment

when he told me I wasn't enough
I believed him

I was taught when I was little
that a kiss would make it better

he was taught this, too

I think we both misunderstood

- every scraped knee

I have starlight in my eyes
a tigress roar that flows from my heart
hips like mirrored crescent moons
and hair like baby's breath

but when he told me my eyes were muddy
I believed him
when he stomped on my heart's voice
I let him
when he told me I take up too much space
my hips swallowed me
when my asymmetrical haircut wasn't feminine to
him anymore
I cried like a baby fighting sleep
like my inner child wanting to be
I cried oceans because I believed him

when he abandoned me in this brokenness
I left myself behind as well
I was trying to go with him
> *why*

I spent countless hours trying to fix a boy
so many minutes sacrificing myself
so many seconds giving all of me until I was barely
breathing

What would happen if I put that effort into loving
myself?

you don't have enough hands
to care for two people
alone

you can't fix him

even if you see the holes in his skin
where the weeds poke through

even if you understand every root in his soil
or think you do

no green thumb can save his wilting flowers
if he himself is not ready to
bloom

you, however, must ask yourself
'Why
are my hands so devoted to his soil
that I am willing to sacrifice
or completely abandon
my own?'

    weed your garden, only yours

don't abandon yourself
by staying with someone you need to
walk away from

when I cry because he left me
I'm also crying because I left myself

the thought of you leaves my stomach
churning, teases my heart
so it beats faster and
melts, dripping to
my gut, leaving
my chest a
hollow
cavity

why is it we spend most of our lives learning...
to love ourselves?

he envied my scent
my floral essence
invited me to grow in his soil
next to him
instead he dug me a hole
and buried me too deep
never to water me
and blocked my path
to the hose

I AM thirsty

I begged him to water me
to bathe me in his sunlight
or to let me go

I could've left at anytime

but my freedom
slowly
became his

discretion

Out of all the people to leave behind,
why would you abandon yourself?

Legality of Lies Pt. 1

What he said,
"I'm not a relationship person."

What he meant,
"Not for you."

fraud by omission

Pt. 2 // Chalk

his fingers were like chalk
and my body was a canvas for his artwork
with hand prints on each breast
and holding both hips

my back was a mural
with streaks
that mimicked butterfly wings
and
soon I was covered
with his residue
smothered
in his finger prints

with every inch of me kissed
and no skin untouched
I was no longer a canvas
but became an asphalt street
driven over
driven through
and driven past

I was promised a nail
a spot on the wall
the potential of a gallery
and the eyes of an art enthusiast

I was given a back alley
untitled
choking on chalk
and cigarette smoke

waiting
and praying
for rain

fraud by misrepresentation

If I feared self doubt as much as I feared my power
I would be unstoppable

I'm hurting from his cruelty
but I realized
I'm just as cruel
to myself

reflections

Self-abandoning will never heal your
dis ease
only presence
and self compassion
can do that

-    return

this
S.exually
T.ransmitted
D.eceit
does not make me
poisonous

- a loving reminder

herpes herpes herpes herpes herpes herpes herpes herpes
herpes herpes herpes herpes herpes herpes herpes herpes
herpes herpes herpes herpes herpes herpes herpes herpes
herpes herpes herpes herpes herpes herpes herpes herpes
herpes herpes herpes herpes herpes herpes herpes herpes
herpes herpes herpes herpes herpes herpes herpes herpes
herpes herpes herpes herpes herpes herpes herpes herpes
herpes herpes herpes herpes herpes herpes herpes herpes
herpes herpes herpes herpes herpes herpes herpes herpes
herpes herpes herpes herpes herpes herpes herpes herpes
herpes herpes herpes herpes herpes herpes herpes herpes
herpes herpes herpes herpes herpes herpes herpes herpes
herpes herpes herpes herpes herpes herpes herpes herpes
herpes herpes herpes herpes herpes herpes herpes herpes
herpes herpes herpes herpes herpes herpes herpes herpes
herpes herpes herpes herpes herpes herpes herpes herpes
herpes herpes herpes herpes herpes herpes herpes herpes
herpes herpes herpes herpes herpes herpes herpes herpes
herpes herpes herpes herpes herpes herpes herpes herpes
herpes herpes herpes herpes herpes herpes herpes herpes
herpes herpes herpes herpes herpes herpes herpes herpes
herpes herpes herpes herpes herpes herpes herpes herpes
herpes herpes herpes herpes herpes herpes herpes herpes
herpes herpes herpes herpes herpes herpes herpes herpes
herpes herpes herpes herpes herpes herpes herpes herpes
herpes herpes herpes herpes herpes herpes herpes herpes
herpes herpes herpes herpes herpes herpes herpes herpes
herpes herpes herpes herpes herpes herpes herpes herpes
herpes herpes herpes herpes herpes herpes herpes herpes
herpes herpes herpes herpes herpes herpes herpes herpes
herpes herpes herpes herpes herpes herpes herpes herpes
herpes herpes herpes herpes herpes herpes herpes herpes
herpes herpes herpes herpes herpes herpes herpes herpes
herpes herpes herpes herpes herpes herpes herpes herpes
herpes herpes herpes herpes herpes herpes herpes herpes
herpes herpes herpes herpes herpes herpes herpes herpes
herpes herpes herpes herpes herpes herpes herpes herpes

herpes herpes herpes herpes herpes herpes herpes herpes
herpes herpes herpes herpes herpes herpes herpes herpes
herpes herpes herpes herpes herpes herpes herpes herpes
herpes herpes herpes herpes herpes herpes herpes herpes
herpes herpes herpes herpes herpes herpes herpes herpes
herpes herpes herpes herpes herpes herpes herpes herpes
herpes herpes herpes herpes herpes herpes herpes herpes
herpes herpes herpes herpes herpes herpes herpes herpes
herpes herpes herpes herpes herpes herpes herpes herpes
herpes herpes herpes herpes herpes herpes herpes herpes
herpes herpes herpes herpes herpes herpes herpes herpes
herpes herpes herpes herpes herpes herpes herpes herpes
herpes herpes herpes herpes herpes herpes herpes herpes
herpes herpes herpes herpes herpes herpes herpes herpes
herpes herpes herpes herpes herpes herpes herpes herpes
herpes herpes herpes herpes herpes herpes herpes herpes
herpes herpes herpes herpes herpes herpes herpes herpes
herpes herpes herpes herpes herpes herpes herpes herpes
herpes herpes herpes herpes herpes herpes herpes herpes
herpes herpes herpes herpes herpes herpes herpes herpes
herpes herpes herpes herpes herpes herpes herpes herpes
herpes herpes herpes herpes herpes herpes herpes herpes
herpes herpes herpes herpes herpes herpes herpes herpes
herpes herpes herpes herpes herpes herpes herpes herpes

how many times do I need to say it
to make it taste like cardboard
and drip like honey
from my lips?

HSV2 still sounds prettier to me

- "herpes"

It was more than swapping spit
and less than two naked souls dancing with their lips
these kisses were somewhere in between
sweet,
new,
and testing the waters

but as our bodies began to heat up
cozy and sweaty like a natural hot spring
I knew it was time to tell him
of my volcanic activity
and the blistering magma
that will soon scab over
but will also return

-    to speak of the risk

I AM lovable
I AM sexy
I AM desirable

-   mantras
    for those with an unwelcomed guest
    who's made their body
    its new
    residence

look at yourself
in the mirror
every day

stare into your pupils
at the smudged makeup on your waterline

watch your hips swing as they dance
and your belly shake

pull apart your lips
and look at your gums, the back of your throat

touch yourself
to your reflection
get off *to* you and *by* you
cum to your beauty

come back
to who you are

Self abandonment is my image of perfection that I
will never
Be.

Perfect
that very idea
and what it looks like to you
seems to be like a pristinely wrapped Christmas
present

Perfect is the illusion
the wrapping paper
but the gift inside is self abandonment
and you leave yourself every calendar year
only returning on the holidays

self abandon, return, self abandon, return, self abandon, return, self abandon, return, self abandon, return,

the cycle, until I learn to stay

the way he treated me was disgusting
almost as disgusting as I was

to myself

If I feared shrinking as much as I feared taking up
space
I would be effervescent

you left me
and I found myself
you returned
and I left myself again

I followed you

why do I do that

BLOCKED

I've meticulously built
concrete walls
six feet thick
towering up and around
the space I require to live
just to keep your
toxic but sometimes alluring
energy
your sloppily written
apologies
your arrogant
fragrance
and belittling touch
very far
away from me

so please tell me
why
I still ache
inside my perfectly insulated
you proofed home
and
my mind keeps searching for traces of
your sincerity
and
my morning eyes wake to your ghost
in bed sometimes *after a dream of you*
and

my lips quiver when I think of kissing
someone new *I know that's never been hard for you
to do*
and
my heart guiltily longs for the idea
of you
still

silently lingering
like my index finger going numb
from clicking
Spam

I don't want to look anymore

I want to get to a place where I no longer
write about
you

when

where

what

who

do you use to self
abandon?

hungry

cook my food on high
feed it to me steaming
with the bottom of the plate too hot to touch bare
handed
make it so I burn my tongue on every bite
maybe then I'll only eat what I'm hungry for

cover my food in Siracha
suffocate it in pepper flakes
load it with Carolina Reapers
burning my mouth and making me sweat
so spicy it turns my face red
maybe then I'll only eat what I'm hungry for

replace the microwave buttons with razor blades
cover the fridge in Creeping Juniper
making it a thorny beast
pricking and stabbing me with each visit
dying my cravings blue in association
they say blue is an unappetizing color
and maybe then I'll only eat what I'm hungry for

very aware of portion sizes
making sure never to exceed this limit in public
even putting at least 1/3 of my meal in a to go box
only to think about it on and off all evening
and eating it all on the way home, alone in my car
maybe even stopping for dessert
being proud if I wait until I'm home to take the first
bite
I don't want you to know I eat more than I'm hungry
for

in a world where it's more attractive to be thin
calling me fat will cut me deeper than almost any
other word
and if you say I'm not, I'll know you're lying
I eat more than I'm hungry for

please understand –
binge eating is a disorder, too
I'm digesting the pantry and not the turmoil of my
heart

my healing is a spiral of weight gain
making my body bigger because I feel so small
and hating the extra flesh

so feed me with a spoon made of spikes
let it slice my tongue to shreds
tomato soup – extra salty so it stings
to the point where I can't distinguish the taste of soup
and blood
then let me wash it down with a mug of hot lemon
water
so the wounds throb in pain

feed me raw chicken
salmon that's gone bad
macaroni and cheese 2 months old
give me food poisoning
so I vomit for days
maybe then I'll only eat what I'm hungry for

Out of all the people who have left me behind
I've abandoned myself the most

what is this voice, this tugging, this darkness, this

habitual cycle?

who & what is this voice that preaches self denial and

worships self doubt?

if you're anything like me, you know it all too well

Let's call it...

DELORIS IS THAT PERFECT IMAGE OF BEAUTY AND GRACE THAT YOU WILL NEVER LIVE UP TO. DELORIS GIVES YOUR POWER AWAY TO ANYONE WHO WILL TAKE IT. DELORIS TELLS YOU THAT YOU'RE NOT GOOD ENOUGH AND THAT YOU SHOULD ALWAYS BE DOING MORE. DELORIS SEEKS APPROVAL OUTISIDE OF YOU. DELORIS IS SHEDDING YOUR SKINS AND SIZE TO SHRINK FOR EVERYONE WHO HAS TOLD YOU THAT YOU ARE TOO MUCH TO HANDLE. DELORIS IS JUDGEMENTAL. SHE'S CRUEL TO YOU IN THE MIRROR AND ON A LONELY SATURDAY NIGHT. DELORIS IS SELF ABANDONMENT. SELF ABANDONMENT IS BEING OVER APOLOGETIC OR APOLOGIZING FOR THE SPACE YOU TAKE UP. DELORIS IS AS SMALL AS SAYING SORRY TO EVERYTHING... EVEN THINGS YOU DIDN'T DO OR WEREN'T YOUR FAULT LIKE SOMEONE BUMPING INTO

YOU AT THE GROCERY STORE. SELF ABANDONMENT IS AS BIG AS REALIZING YOU WERE RAPED A YEAR AFTER IT HAPPENED BECAUSE YOU TOLD YOURSELF YOU WERE OVER REACTING. DELORIS BELIEVES YOU CAN'T ACCOMPLISH YOUR DREAMS. SELF ABANDONMENT IS ADDICTION AND KEEEPING YOU DISTRACTED FROM YOUR INNER YOU. DELORIS BELIEVES YOU NEED SOMEONE OR SOMETHING ELSE TO MAKE YOU WHOLE. DELORIS BELIEVES THAT EVERYONE ELSE KNOWS BETTER THAN YOU DO. SELF ABANDONMENT IS BEING IN AN ABUSIVE RELATIONSHIP. DELORIS QUESTIONS YOUR WORTH AND BELIEVES YOU'RE A BURDEN. SELF ABANDONMENT IS WHY YOU'RE ALWAYS LOOKING....SEARCHING....FOR SOMETHING...YOU'RE LOOKING FOR YOU.

MAYBE YOU LEFT HER A LONG TIME AGO OR MAYBE

YOU'RE IN AND OUT LIKE A NETFLIX EPISODE

BUFFERING EVERY 15 FUCKING MINUTES OR MAYBE

WITH PRACTICE YOU'VE GOTTEN GOOD AT STAYING.

WHEREVER YOU ARE – YOU CAN ALWAYS RETURN

HOME. YOU CAN ALWAYS RETURN TO YOU. PLACE YOUR

RIGHT HAND OVER YOUR HEART AND HOLD YOUR LEFT

HAND UP TO THE SKY. EMBRACE YOUR INNERCHILD

AND PLAY WITH GLITTER OR CHALK OR PUT STICKERS

ALL OVER YOUR STEERING WHEEL TO REMIND YOU

EVERY DAY TO PLAY WITH LIFE'S PLEASURES. DANCE

NAKED IN YOUR ROOM ATLEAST ONCE A WEEK AND

DON'T LET THE SHAKING OF YOUR BELLY AFFECT HOW

MUCH YOU EAT THE NEXT DAY. TAKE UP SPACE,

STRETCH OUT YOUR ARMS, YOUR LEGS, YOUR HEART,

AND SING.

DO YOU FEEL HOME IN YOUR BODY AND THE LOVE IN YOUR HEART? TELL DELORIS THAT SHE IS NO LONGER WELCOME THERE.

TELL DELORIS THAT YOU NO LONGER BELIEVE HER. SHE IS NO LONGER WELCOME IN YOU OR IN YOUR COMPANY.

COME BACK TO WHO YOU ARE. STAND IN YOUR POWER. SWIM IN YOUR STRENGTH. DANCE IN YOUR SELF LOVE. BREATHE IN THE COSMIC WAVE AND LET DELORIS GO WITH THE WIND. BREAK THE AGREEMENT. STEP INTO YOUR FREEDOM. SING LOUD.

Deloris started as a metaphor for different aspects of cheating & being cheated on in a relationship.

This is what Deloris has evolved into becoming.

DEFINITION

Deloris
/duh-lohr-ris/
Noun

1.   his wandering eye

2.   the other girls

3.   the parts of you that accepted shitty treatment, the parts of you that believe(d) and agree(d) to abusive language

4.   anywhere, anything, or anyone you use to self abandon

I'm trying
with all the might and fire in my belly
to break this habit

like a planking exercise
I'm going strong
until I'm burning
until I cave in

and I collapse
onto the cold floor with bare skin

returning

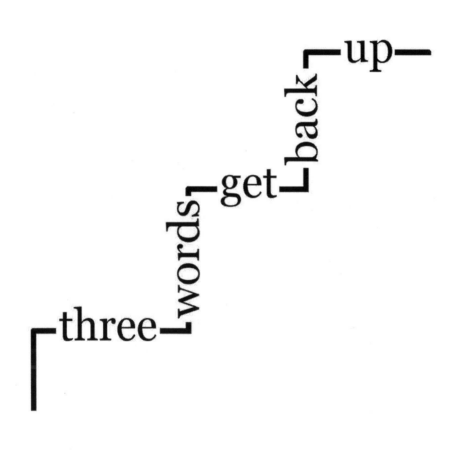

the first step to healing

this habit

is returning

return to who you are

to your truth

reclaim your true spirit

keep trying

return to *you* every time you wake from the illusion

thank the condensed water
that causes fog
makes clarity all the clearer

forgive unfairness
let go of what you do not condone
make freedom your new mirror

with rise and fall
we learn the laws of gravity
making balance so much dearer

remember,
there is no separate god above us
for we are a cup of divine love
if that love were an ocean

remember,
through the mud blooms the lotus
you dive into all that you are
not by skipping stones on the surface

when you return to yourself
your heart flutters like

butterfly wings

saying, "Welcome home."

when you return to yourself
you open your arms to the cosmic wave
to the loving light's ever present hug

every cell in your body bathes
in grace
in healing
in sacred song

you're always welcome here

Home

it's not a place
nor a person

Home

is in your heart
and only you can move away

don't ever make a man your brick and mortar

I've made pillows
out of the hearts of my old lovers
and bed frames
from the strength of their shoulders
but
not this time
not with him

slowly
we are building a fire
and
getting to know
the flames

slowly

slower

slow

his heart was my pillow
for the night
but
I know now
where my home is
and when to go
camping

-   *sleepovers*

don't keep the blinds closed
only shut your eyelids to rest
at night

wake with the sunrise
breathe in the sunshine
eyes open
heart open wider

receive

I realized
most of my loneliness stems from
abandoning myself

stay to blossom

let me love my deepest insides
from my roots
to my ovaries
to each budding petal

let me love
from seed
to bloom

blossoming

break me open
let me get to know the strength
of my pistil
the core of my female embodiment
the center of my femininity
my connection to the goddess collective

I AM
woman

I AM
womb-an

I AM
birthing new life
and new love
into my heart
supporting my sisters also in bloom

Cosmic Mother,
break us open
so we get to intimately know the strength
of our pistils

they're far more powerful than any gun

self love is evergreen
everlasting all seasons
even winter

summer
fall
winter
spring

I AM
always

free

to choose again

we go through

seasons

in our love

and

in our art

we grow though

seasons

and so

we come

to know our heart

Sometimes
you have to burn
before you can

RISE

-phoenix

I have died many times
shed many skins
and today I mourn my own death
knowing I will rise
   -   again & again

instead of drowning in self judgment
soar in self praise

self love grows wings

some may tell you to sit down
to be quiet
to be still as to not ruffle any

feathers

ignore them
show them how beautifully feathers can fly

out of gas
with a flat tire
I thought I could go no further

then the blades in my shoulders
with a sharp persistence
and the grace of a feather floating in the wind
slowly funneled into the becoming
of wings
and I flew to new heights

I AM
thankful
for the second wind

I AM
grateful
for feet
and for flight

meet yourself where you are
         not where you want to be

I'm learning to trust
to stay trusting

-   the universe provides

I'm leaking

and I don't have enough hands to cover every hole,

every vacancy that I carry

I'm leaking

spilling out my sweetness and oozing out my radiance

I'm leaking

from the wound in my back heart

the gaping hole in my stomach

this slit throat

the blistered anger

the gash on my side

I'm leaking

and no cork top or warm lips could seal these wounds

no night of sleep could rest these tired bones quite

enough

and chocolate has lost its taste

But oh my,

how have I forgotten?

the sweet kiss of warm grass beneath bare feet

the way the sun can hug your whole being in an
instant
the medicine of an animal's presence
the psalms in my very palms
the healing power of self love

I'm healing
and my leaking parts are being kissed with divine
love, angels' wings, and mother nature
I'm healing
as I breathe into my growth
as I breathe into my budding
as I breathe into my blossoming
as I breathe into change
as I breathe out all that I no longer need
as I breathe out all that serves me no more
as I breathe out resistance
and breathe into acceptance

I'm healing
And I'm right where I need to be

   always

returning to yourself is
messy and
beautiful
like a child,
you start jumping in puddles
but of your own rain
and dance so hard you lose your balance
knowing it will find you again
like the four leaf clovers always do

don't you ever mistake my softness as weakness
in vulnerability there is great strength

life is messy

get your hands dirty

walk to your car when it's raining and let your tongue catch the
blessings of the clouds

life is messy

so walk barefoot more often

and let your boobs hang freely *when* you feel like it and
wherever you feel like it

life is messy

and sometimes the dishes can wait until the morning

and the laundry will pile high

and that is *okay*

life is messy

and in your strides to be neat

be sure to let your hair down every once in a while, too

and paint with the mess

make art out of it

let your senses be ravenous

treat your life like a great art project

never quite orderly

but the mess is magical

and it sparkles

like the glitter you wore last Tuesday and still find on your
swept floors

once I looked in the mirror
and realized I was not
poisonous
that was the day
I started to fall back in love
with me and my sensuality

once I looked at the blistered anger
in compassion and with acceptance
that was the day
I realized my hate for the outbreaks
would only enflame it

once I began to love myself
as I am
wherever I am
with whatever circumstance
my heart opened

I am not poison
I am the essence of glitter
the taste of a turmeric tonic
an elixr of a human
and once I could see that

I stopped attracting bugs
and blistered bees

he moaned when I ran my hand
along his chest
I wonder,
if it was his heart's cry
to be loved
and freed from the fear
to open again

   -   courtesy of his ex lover

crazy

how trauma
unites us

and tears us apart
just the same

he placed his hand
on my back
behind my heart
my personal ruin

I told him it was *the stabbing place*
he said, *not anymore*

he doesn't know

my trauma
rests in me like
landmines

the ticking
keeps me up
at night

and his fingers
flirt with my fear
of loss

I am learning
to dismantle my instinct
to flinch
to run
to hide away
in the scars on my
skin

I am beginning to
trust

-   *new love*

my heart
has been longing
for a new chest
to beat against

he is warm
and not a maze to get lost in
but instead I'm finding new parts
of myself

his sweetness
is thick as honey
so I'm tasting it slowly
knowing he's not going anywhere
anytime soon

and his palms are
soft
he has gentle hands
not fists
so I'm learning not to
flinch
when he brushes my hair
from my
eyes

Sadie

10 years old

sweet and sassy

like a glass of lemonade

made a friend out of me in the waiting room

her mother returned

apologized for her chattiness

immediately told me *she talks too much*

THIS

is why we lose our voice

stop apologizing for who you are

you are *always* enough, you are *always* enough, you are *always* enough

you are *always* enough, you are *always* enough, you are *always* enough

you are *always* enough, you are *always* enough, you are *always* enough

you are *always* enough, you are *always* enough, you are *always* enough

you are *always* enough, you are *always* enough, you are *always* enough

you are *always* enough, you are *always* enough, you are *always* enough

you are *always* enough, you are *always* enough, you are *always* enough

you are *always* enough, you are *always* enough, you are *always* enough

you are *always* enough, you are *always* enough, you are *always* enough

you are *always* enough, you are *always* enough, you are *always* enough

you are *always* enough, you are *always* enough, you are *always* enough you are *always* enough, you are *always* enough, you are *always* enough

you are *always* enough, you are *always* enough, you are *always* enough

you are *always* enough, you are *always* enough, you are *always* enough

you are *always* enough, you are *always* enough, you are *always* enough

you are *always* enough, you are *always* enough, you are *always* enough

you are *always* enough, you are *always* enough, you are *always* enough

you are *always* enough, you are *always* enough, you are *always* enough

you are *always* enough, you are *always* enough, you are *always* enough

you are *always* enough, you are *always* enough, you are *always* enough

you are *always* enough, you are *always* enough, you are *always* enough

you are *always* enough, you are *always* enough, you are *always* enough

YOU are worthy

you *are*
and will *always* be

In the middle of the night
when you're alone
and feeling
swallowed whole

remind yourself that
you are worth staying for

always

I am trying to untangle

the fingers

that are holding my

tongue

and choking my

voice

why am I so scared to be myself

there is so much

hurt

behind my eyes

and I can't blink it all away

\-   healing takes time

I thought that
returning to myself
would be the needle and thread
to sew my happiness and my wholeness
back together

in many ways this is true

but I forgot the pain of
ripping stitches
and pricked fingers

sometimes

returning feels like

a tub of cold water

a bath you drew for yourself

weeks ago

and watch go down the drain

-   *missed opportunities*

I have been used
many times
as a door mat
or as a cheap love motel

so I've learned from the best
how to leave

- *checking out*

but when he says,
"I love you &
I'm not going anywhere anytime soon."
I believe him.

I'm learning to say this to myself

- *moving in*

MOVE IN

move into your power
into your strength
into your sensuality

MOVE IN

move into transitions
into your desires
into your truth

move into your growth
into your beauty
into self love and compassion

move boldly into your space
into your boundaries
into your inspiration

MOVE IN

and relish in the celebration
&
in the chorus of your heart singing, "Welcome home."

Made in the USA
Columbia, SC
17 February 2025

53943526R00057